THE MI]
WHAT NEW CHRISTIANS NEED TO KNOW

Author
MICK BRINDLE

The Milk of Truth
By Mick Brindle

Unless otherwise noted, Scripture is taken from the HOLY BIBLE NEW INTERNATIONAL VERSION. Copyright© 1973, 1978, 1984 by International Bible Society. Used by permission of Zondervan Publishing House. All rights reserved.

All Rights Reserved. You may use any part of this book in any manner appropriate to build up the body of Christ in an effort to reach unity in the faith and the knowledge of the Son of God attaining the whole measure of the fullness of Christ.

Please note, that the name satan and related names are not capitalized. We choose not to acknowledge him, even to the point of violating grammatical rules.

TABLE OF CONTENTS

Chapter 1
You Can Be Sure   13

Chapter 2
Brown Pastures   21

Chapter 3
Script or Scripture   25

Chapter 4
Lions & Sheep   29

Chapter 5
Doing The Right Thing   35

Chapter 6
Here For A Reason   41

Chapter 7
Putting On The Armor   47

Chapter 8
Keys To Faith   53

Chapter 9
The Hour Of Trial   63

DEDICATION

I have dedicated this book to my sons Mick and Jacob. They both came to know Jesus at a young age and have endured through some difficult times as we traveled around the country with my military career leaving friends and familiar places. They have learned to persevere in their faith and the journey God laid before them. They have made wise decisions in life and the Lord has blessed them tremendously.

My boys, now professional men have always encouraged their mother and me and have treated us with great respect. I do not have the words to describe how proud I am of them and the respect and admiration I have for them as men of strong character. I count it a rare privilege as a father to speak such words about my children. I thank God for my sons and their obedience and yielding to the Lord.

I pray for God's great blessings on the both of you and may He grant you the desires of your heart as you pursue Him.

"The prayer of a righteous man is powerful and effective"

FOREWORD

Becoming a follower of Jesus is "The" most important decision you will ever make in your lifetime. The impact of this decision will literally change your entire way of thinking, living and perspective on life and eternity.

Jesus came so that we might have life in fullness with all the blessings and joy that He has to offer. So great is God's love for humankind that He cannot bear to be apart from us, His children. God made us in His image for relationship. Salvation is not something you can earn, because this is God's gift to you and not by anything you have done on your own. It is given by mercy from God through His son. God planned in the beginning for us to do good things and to live, as He has always wanted us to live. That is why He sent Jesus.

As you grow in your new faith and study the Bible (God's Word), you will find that He has a plan for those He loves. In Ephesians 1, the apostle Paul writes, that in Jesus, we were made as part of Gods heritage, and He gives us an inheritance. We were chosen and appointed beforehand according to His purpose and will.

This is an incredible act of grace on God's part. He made us for a purpose, His purpose. Because we have given our life to Jesus and made Him Lord (ruler) of our life, our purpose is to give honor to God by how we live and serve Him. We have the assurance of knowing that we will receive what God has stored up for each one of us since the beginning of time.

INTRODUCTION

As you read this book, please keep in mind that it is written at a level appropriate for new believers. References to other books and resources are found throughout the book.

I often reflect on and wonder what my life would have been like without Jesus. As I look back to thirty years ago, I did not like the way I once lived as a young man and have many regrets. Frankly, I cannot imagine the prospect of not knowing the Lord and having Him as a major part of my life today. I came to realize that life would be a great struggle without Him.

I remember when I first became a Christian and how I was so full of joy in the Lord that I could hardly contain myself. I remember the next day before I went to work; I stopped at a coffee shop. I was a young man of 19 years wearing an Air Force uniform. The man next to me struck up a conversation as we sat their drinking coffee. I remember I started talking to him about Jesus. I really did not know what to say because I was only one day old in the family of God. I just explained to him what I experienced the day before. He seemed very interested. All I did was share my testimony. (How I received Christ) I didn't know that's what it was. Even so, he let me pray with him before we parted ways. That was the first and only time I saw him there. This memory crosses my mind from time to time. I really think he was an Angel!

I often wonder what happened to that man, or if he really was an Angel. Someday I will find out when I ask the Lord. I can only pray that a seed of faith was planted and the Lord started the growing process. Maybe this seed was meant to be planted in me, to bring about my involvement in so many ministries over these past years. Life is like that sometimes. You may only get one chance to share Jesus with someone. That is why it is so important not to pass up any opportunity to share His love. To share what He has done for us through His son Jesus.

WHAT DO ALL THOSE CHURCH WORDS MEAN?

Anointed: When you pour oil to show that God is choosing a person. "When God Chooses."

Bless: To ask God to do something good or to make "holy."

Christ: Is the "Anointed" one. Messiah, as foretold by the prophets of the Hebrew Scriptures.

Confess: To tell God what you have done wrong and agree with Him that you were wrong.

Covenant (Testament): A very serious agreement.

Disciple: Having someone come along side you showing and teaching you how to be a Christian.

Discernment: To be able to tell the difference between one thing and another.

Faith: Totally believing that something is true even though there maybe no way to prove what you believe is true.

Flesh: The part inside of you that wants to sin.

Glory: Honor and praise.

Grace: Treating someone special when they do not deserve it.

Honor: To treat with great respect.

Holy: Belongs to God and set apart for God.

Humility: To not think more of yourself than you should or what you do.

Lord: Someone who rules – Lord with a capital "L" means ruler of other rulers.

Meat of the word: Deep truths of the Bible – some hard to understand. Like meat, you need to "chew" on.

Milk of the word: The elementary truths regarding the Bible. Easy to understand – Like drinking milk.

Messiah: One who is anticipated as, regarded as, or professes to be a Savior or liberator.

Prophet: A person chosen by God to tell a message from Him.

Redeemed: To set free, rescue or buy back.

Righteousness: What God says is right.

Repent: Turning from your bad behavior to good.

Savior: A person who saves or rescues you.

Sin: When I choose my own way instead of God's way.

The Word: Another way of saying the Bible or Jesus who is the living Word.

Worship: To give your <u>greatest</u> love and honor.

Chapter 1
YOU CAN BE SURE

God is righteous, perfect and infinitely holy. That is His standard. It is called "glory" in the New Testament. Look closely at Ephesians 2:8. Paraphrased it says, "God showed His grace which means "favor" on us. There's nothing we can do to earn God's favor." He is perfect, holy, and righteous. Perfection is His standard.

For it is by grace you have been saved, through faith— and this not from yourselves, it is the gift of God. Ephesians 2:8

Reading these verses, we see that Jesus was our substitute. By receiving Him, we are now favored by God. He is the sinless and perfect Son of God. He is the One who accomplished your rescue. It occurred on the cross. Sin requires a penalty of death in order for God's righteous demands to be satisfied. Jesus fulfilled that requirement to the letter. We have been redeemed (bought back) by the blood of Jesus.

Is there any way for the Christian to lose this gift? No, never! Why? Because if you work for your salvation you can lose it. This is a gift. You cannot turn a gift into a wage. You see, no one can earn the gift of eternal life and no one can ever say how little work is enough to lose it, because a gift is something that cannot be earned. Read Romans 4: 4-5.

One thing you can be sure of is the eternal security of your salvation. When you profess Jesus as your Savior and Lord of your life, the Holy Spirit covers and dwells within you. You become born again and made a new creation in Jesus.

Do you not know that your body is a temple of the Holy Spirit, who is in you, whom you have received from God? You are not your own: 1 Corinthians 6:19

Therefore, if anyone is in Christ, he is a new creation; the old has gone, the new has come! 1 Corinthians 5:7

I know the phrase "born again" sounds very strange to someone who is unfamiliar with Bible teaching. Nevertheless, we must come to realize that the natural man sees everything from an earthly point of view with their natural senses. You must be willing to give up your own point of view, ideas and personal will. This was the case with Nicodemus in John chapter 3 as well. He could not understand how you could be physically born from your mother again. This is not what Jesus was speaking of. He was speaking of a Spiritual rebirth.

Now there was a man of the Pharisees named Nicodemus, a member of the Jewish ruling council. He came to Jesus at night and said, "Rabbi, we know you are a teacher who has come from God. For no one could perform the miraculous signs you are doing if God were not with him."

In reply Jesus declared, "I tell you the truth, no one can see the kingdom of God unless he is born again."

"How can a man be born when he is old?" Nicodemus asked. "Surely he cannot enter a second time into his mother's womb to be born!"

Jesus answered, "I tell you the truth, no one can enter the kingdom of God unless he is born of water and the Spirit. Flesh gives birth to flesh, but the Spirit gives birth to spirit. You should not be surprised at my saying, 'You must be born again.'

The wind blows wherever it pleases. You hear its sound, but you cannot tell where it comes from or where it is going. So it is with everyone born of the Spirit." John 3: 1-8

For God, who said, "Let light shine out of darkness," made his light shine in our hearts to give us the light of the knowledge of the glory of God in the face of Christ. 2 Corinthians 4:6

REBIRTH

You see, Nicodemus was looking at rebirth from a purely physical perspective, from his natural mind. Jesus was speaking from a heavenly or spiritual context. Those who have not received Jesus do not have the indwelling Holy Spirit and cannot understand the things of God. The Holy Spirit is not something you see, but "someone" you have a relationship with that guides you in every thought and deed as your will allows.

And whatever you do, whether in word or deed, do it all in the name of the Lord Jesus, giving thanks to God the Father through him. Colossians 3:17

However, as it is written: "No eye has seen, no ear has heard, no mind has conceived what God has prepared for those who love him", but God has revealed it to us by his Spirit. The Spirit searches all things, even the deep things of God. For who among men knows the thoughts of a man except the man's spirit within him? 1 Corinthians 2: 9-11

Many people think that for someone to get into heaven it takes a little luck or doing a greater number of good things in life than bad. I know I once thought that way. Most people know deep within them, there is something more after this life. Many think they may come back as someone or something else after death. You know what, they are right about one thing. There is more to life than just the present. There is eternity! In eternity, there are only two choices. You are with God or without Him.

I know that sounds very blunt, but the only way to God the Father is through Jesus Christ. God sent His only son to die on a cross as an "offering" for our sins. In other words, Jesus paid the price of sin with His very life, so we can be forgiven and spend eternity with Him.

Jesus answered, "I am the way and the truth and the life. No one comes to the Father except through me". John 14:6

For God so loved the world that he gave his one and only Son, that whoever believes in him shall not perish but have eternal life. For God did not send his Son into the world to condemn the world, but to save the world through him. John 3: 16-17

One thing we need to understand, is that forgiveness is given when you repent, (which means to turn away from your old lifestyle of sin) and in faith receive Jesus Christ. Salvation then becomes instant and with it comes the forgiveness of sin. It is not a matter of changing behavior, but a matter of the heart. God loves willing hearts and the Holy Spirit will change your behavior as you grow in your Christian walk. Matters of the heart are of the highest importance to God. There are over 540 references to the heart in the Bible.

But the Counselor, the Holy Spirit, whom the Father will send in my name, will teach you all things and will remind you of everything I have said to you. Luke 14:26

And you, my son Solomon, acknowledge the God of your father, and serve him with wholehearted devotion and with

a willing mind, for the LORD searches every heart and understands every motive behind the thoughts. If you seek him, he will be found by you; but if you forsake him, he will reject you forever. **1 Chronicles 28:9**

BAPTISM

Baptism is not a necessity to secure your newfound salvation. However, when you surrender your heart and life to Jesus, baptism is a sign or an act of identification with Him. Consider the thief on the cross that acknowledged Jesus as the Savior. Jesus said that this man would be with Him in paradise. Did the thief have the opportunity for baptism? No, he did not. However, his salvation was secure.

Jesus answered him, "I tell you the truth, today you will be with me in paradise." Luke 23:43

It must be clearly understood that the true sign of belonging to Jesus is not baptism, but the evidence of Him living in and through your life. This is called the fruit of the Spirit. I will cover this more in later chapters.

Immersion in baptism is a symbol of Christ's death, burial, and resurrection. This act is a testimony that shows being buried in the likeness of His death, to the old sin nature, and raised to the newness of life in the salvation of Christ.

Or don't you know that all of us who were baptized into Christ Jesus were baptized into his death? Romans 6:3

Baptism for those who hear and accept with a simple understanding of the truth, realize first, that we are sinners by nature. Second, that Jesus died on the cross for our sin, and third, that we are convinced of our need for Him as our personal Savior and Lord.

The Bible reveals clearly that salvation is not a matter of man's mind approving certain facts, but rather a person is saved by surrendering his heart to God in a simple child-like faith. Jesus said:

"I tell you the truth, unless you change and become like little children, you will never enter the kingdom of heaven. Matthew 18:3

In conclusion, we clearly see that baptism is simply identifying ourselves with Jesus after receiving Him as our Savior. As you read this, please bear in mind that you may have been sprinkled as a child or immersed as an adult, but unless your heart is utterly yielded to Jesus at this very moment, you are still a lost soul. If this is the case, make it right with God right now by praying this prayer and meaning it from your heart.

That if you confess with your mouth, "Jesus is Lord," and believe in your heart that God raised him from the dead, you will be saved. Romans 10:9

"Lord Jesus Christ, I realize I am a sinner. I believe you died and shed your blood for <u>my</u> sins. I believe you were raised from the dead. I know I have eternal life in you. Right now, I turn from my sin and ask you to come into my life. I receive you as my personal Savior and Lord. Amen."

JUST THE FACTS:
- ✓ Being born again is an act of child like faith.
- ✓ Salvation is a gift and cannot be earned.
- ✓ Baptism identifies you with the death, burial, and resurrection of Jesus.
- ✓ Baptism does not get you into heaven.
- ✓ God is interested in your heart.

My Thoughts:

_____

_____

_____

_____

_____

_____

_____

_____

Chapter 2
BROWN PASTURES

Have you ever heard the saying that the grass is always greener on the other side? This is a deceptive statement and a metaphor that has different meanings to people in their circumstance or condition. Often times we do not realize that the grass or pastures we live in are actually green right now. It is when we make hasty decisions in times of temptation or distress that turn the grass brown. You are probably wondering what I mean by that!

Let us look at a story in the first book of the Bible, Genesis Chapter 2. Here we see Adam living in this beautiful Garden in Eden. Life is grand for him at this point. God planted all kinds of trees pleasing to the eye with fruit that he could eat from except for one. In the middle of the garden stood the tree of life and the tree of the knowledge of good and evil. God said he was not to eat from the tree of the knowledge of good and evil because if he did, he would die. Well it would seem to me that is clear.

However, God was not speaking about immediate physical death. He was referring to a gradual death living life exposed to temptation and sin. If Adam had not eaten from the forbidden tree, he would not have died, because the sinful nature of man would still be absent in the world. You see, sin brings spiritual and physical death.

[Death Through Adam, Life Through Christ] Therefore, just as sin entered the world through one man, and death through sin, and in this way death came to all men, because all sinned. Romans 5:12

For the wages of sin is death, but the gift of God is eternal life in Christ Jesus our Lord. Romans 6:23

God was also talking about a relationship death. You see, the close relationship Adam had with God would no longer be there. By this I mean, Adam would be eternally separated from God because He (God) cannot look upon sin.

Surely the arm of the LORD is not too short to save, nor his ear too dull to hear. But your iniquities have separated you from your God; your sins have hidden his face from you, so that he will not hear. Isaiah 53: 1-2

THE FALL OF MAN

As we look further in Genesis, we see the fall of man and woman. Now God said that it was not good for Adam to be alone. As a result, He caused a deep sleep to fall on Adam and God removed one of his ribs to make woman as a helpmate and to be a companion. God then brought the woman to Adam.

For this reason a man will leave his father and mother and be united to his wife, and they will become one flesh. **Genesis 2:24**

Husbands, love your wives, just as Christ loved the church and gave himself up for her. **Ephesians 5:25**

Husbands, love your wives and do not be harsh with them. **Colossians 3:19**

They both knew not to eat from the forbidden tree. Even so, there was another in the garden, the serpent. The serpent (satan) said to Eve, "Did God really say that, you must not eat from the tree?" The serpent persuaded her into picking the fruit from the forbidden tree. The serpent in his sly and seductive manner said to Eve, "you will not die", your eyes will be open, and you will be like God".

Doesn't this sound familiar? It's because the nature of man is so self-centered that we are continually trying to be something greater than ourselves. We must be constantly on our guard, especially as new believers to the subtle deception of the serpent.

Consequently, Eve was seduced into thinking the fruit was good and pleasing to look at and desirable for gaining wisdom. As a result, both she and Adam knowing full well what God said, both rebelled and ate the fruit.

When they ate the fruit their eyes were opened. They were both ashamed that they were naked and sewed leaves together for a covering. Ever since, humans have been "hiding" from each other and from God. As a result, they were expelled from the garden and from the presence of God. Their fall into sin left humanity without the hope of heaven apart from a new birth.

> JUST THE FACTS:
> - ✓ Adam's sin separated everyone from God.
> - ✓ God cannot look at sin.
> - ✓ God desires a relationship with us.
> - ✓ Married couples should honor and love each other as Christ loves us.
> - ✓ Our hope is in Jesus Christ.

My Thoughts:

___

___

___

___

___

Chapter 3
SCRIPT OR SCRIPTURE

How do we know the events and places revealed in the Bible are even real? How do you prove the authenticity of the Bible? This has been a point many scholars have tried to refute for centuries. The best position for proof is in the original documents (manuscripts) that validate existing writings. In this case, existing Bible manuscripts. I don't want to get too deep into this subject, but I think it is necessary to throw out some facts that validate the truth.

I can guarantee that at some time in your Christian walk you will run into someone that will tell you there is no way you can prove the Bible is true. Knowing some basic facts about the Bible will help tremendously when you start sharing the truth. Let's take a look.

PROVE IT!

One of the most important factors to proving authenticity is by the original written works or the transmitted replication of those works. Thousands of years ago, people did not have the advantage of the technology as we do today. Most documents were written on animal hides as with the original writings of the Bible. However, there was a group of priests that dedicated their lives generation after generation to the precise replication of the original manuscripts. As you can imagine this was a slow and methodical process with painstaking checks to ensure the near perfect re-transcription of these documents. Without question, the integrity and context of the original writings were preserved.

It is now known that there are more than 5,300 Greek manuscripts of the New Testament. In addition; over 10,000 Latin Vulgate and 9,300 other early versions. We have more than 24,000 manuscript copies of many portions of the New Testament in existence today. No other document of ancient origin even comes close to approaching such numbers to validate their authenticity.

The only writing existing today, that comes next in line to the greatest number of transmitted documents to validate authenticity, is the Iliad by Homer. It was written in 900 B.C with 643 validation writings. As you can see, the written evidence for the Bible is overwhelming. Further solidifying the Bible's reliability is the archeological evidence, the cross-referencing of prophecies, people, and places. These were all foretold in the Old Testament coming to fulfillment in the New. The sheer numbers of the transmitted documents solidifies the validation of the Bible as an accurate historical writing.

As you can see, the written transmissions, spoken, and prophetic evidence is very difficult to refute when it comes to the authenticity of God's written Word. I have only touched the surface of this subject. To study this subject more in depth, read "A Ready Defense" by Josh McDowell.

Unique among all the books ever written, the Bible accurately foretells specific events in detail many years, sometimes centuries, before they occurred. Approximately 2500 prophecies appear in the pages of the Bible, about 2000 of which have been fulfilled to the letter without error. The remaining 500 reach into the future and may be seen unfolding as days go by especially in the Middle East. The probability for any one of these prophecies having been fulfilled by chance averages less than one in ten (figured very conservatively). Since the prophecies are for the most part independent of one another, the odds for all these prophecies having been fulfilled by chance without error is less than one in 102000 (that is a 1 with 2000 zeros written after it)

THE BOTTOM LINE

As you can see, the evidence is substantial. Those that would argue about the reliability of the Bible are those who are not willing to admit the condition and position of their own soul. Paul makes it clear in Romans 1.

The wrath of God is being revealed from heaven against all the godlessness and wickedness of men who suppress the truth by their wickedness, since what may be known about God is plain to them, because God has made it plain to them.

For since the creation of the world God's invisible qualities—his eternal power and divine nature—have been clearly seen, being understood from what has been made, so that men are without excuse. **Romans 1: 18-20**

    Paul explains that man in his inner consciousness is aware of God, because He has shown Himself to them since the creation of the world. God's invisible nature and attributes, His eternal power and divinity are understood by the existence of all that is created. That sounds pretty deep and complicated right. In other words, His hand is evident in the complexity of creation; it did not happen by chance, it was intelligently designed.

JUST THE FACTS:
- ✓ You must know what you believe.
- ✓ We are called to share the Gospel.
- ✓ The Bible's authenticity is the greatest ever documented.
- ✓ We know the reality of God by His creation.

My Thoughts:

Chapter 4
LIONS & SHEEP

When we first become followers of Jesus and are new in our faith, we are very vulnerable. Just as an infant is very dependent upon its parents, we are dependent on the Holy Spirit as our guide through life.

You may not know this, but satan goes around like a lion hunting his prey, especially Christians. When you are not a follower of Jesus, satan is content with you living in your current condition of darkness and sin, because he knows you are deceived. However, when you become a believer in Jesus, satan now hunts you with the intent of destroying your faith and obedience.

Be self-controlled and alert. Your enemy the devil prowls around like a roaring lion looking for someone to devour. Resist him, standing firm in the faith, because you know that your brothers throughout the world are undergoing the same kind of sufferings. 1 Peter 5: 8-9

This is why it is very important to attend a church with those who encourage one another and teach the truth of the Bible. There is great strength, protection, and wisdom within a congregation of strong Christ following believers.

Find out what type of classes and discipleship training are available. I would highly recommend that you spend at least one year being discipled (learning about God) and encouraged by mature believers.

KNOWING HIS VOICE

The remarkable thing about the Holy Spirit is He reveals the things of God to us as we pursue Him. The Holy Spirit searches and examines all things. He reveals the unexplainable things of God and teaches us the hidden meaning of these things that are beyond man's understanding.

You see, once we receive the Holy Spirit it is God's desire and deep pleasure to bless (things God does for you) us and give us His gifts. When we were without Jesus in our natural condition, we could not accept or even understand the things of God. They were meaningless and nonsense to us, even at times offensive.

Nevertheless, once we have the Holy Spirit within us, our inner spirit examines, investigates, and questions all things. As a result, we receive insight from God on how to apply it to daily living. No man fully understands the counsel and purposes of the Lord. His followers are renewed in their minds daily and become aware of His thoughts, feelings and purposes revealed in His heart for each of us.

However, as it is written: "No eye has seen, no ear has heard, no mind has conceived what God has prepared for those who love him," but God has revealed it to us by his Spirit. 1 Corinthians 2: 9-10.

THE GOOD SHEPHERD

Jesus is the good Shepherd. He spoke often in parables (stories) so the people of the time could understand and apply it to the life they lived. Jesus is the gate to salvation. He is the innocent lamb, God's only Son sent to give His life as a ransom (payment) for all sins. Once you receive Jesus, you have entered through the gate and are now one of His sheep.

If you know anything about the behavior of sheep, you might understand that they need leading. As the shepherd leads his sheep, they come to know him by his manner and voice as he speaks and instructs them daily. It is the same with us. As we grow in our relationship with Jesus, we become very familiar with our heavenly shepherd, and He knows us by name. The flock will not follow or obey the commands of a stranger. They run from him because they sense danger in a strange voice. This is the same with us. The thief (satan) comes to steal, kill and destroy.

"I tell you the truth, the man who does not enter the sheep pen by the gate, but climbs in by some other way, is a thief and a robber. The man who enters by the gate is the shepherd of his sheep. The watchman opens the gate for him, and the sheep listen to his voice. He calls his own sheep by name and leads them out. When he has brought out all his own, he goes on ahead of them, and his sheep follow him because they know his voice. But they will never follow a stranger; in fact, they will run away from him because they do not recognize a stranger's voice." Jesus used this figure of speech, but they did not understand what he was telling them.

> The Simple Truth: As you pursue Christ, your relationship grows with greater intimacy. You will not only with certainty know the sound of His voice, but will recognize the gentle unspoken desires He has on the path of life set before you.

Therefore Jesus said again, "I tell you the truth, I am the gate for the sheep. All who ever came before me were thieves and robbers, but the sheep did not listen to them. I am the gate; whoever enters through me will be saved. He will come in and go out, and find pasture. The thief comes only to steal and kill and destroy; I have come that they may have life, and have it to the full.

"I am the good shepherd. The good shepherd lays down his life for the sheep. The hired hand is not the shepherd who owns the sheep. So when he sees the wolf coming, he abandons the sheep and runs away.

Then the wolf attacks the flock and scatters it. The man runs away because he is a hired hand and cares nothing for the sheep. John 10: 1-12

Make sure you listen to the right shepherd. There are many false teachers out there. The deceiver (satan) goes around as a ravenous wolf in sheep's clothing. If what is said does not line up with the Word of God, reject it!

"Beware of the false prophets, who come to you in sheep's clothing, but inwardly are ravenous wolves. Mathew 7:15

JUST THE FACTS:
- ✓ Satan wants to destroy your faith in Jesus.
- ✓ Jesus is our Shepherd.
- ✓ We must know His voice.
- ✓ Beware of false teachers.

My Thoughts:

_____

_____

_____

_____

_____

_____

Chapter 5
DOING THE RIGHT THING

As I stated earlier, becoming a new believer has new challenges. The things you once did and the friendships you had may cause conflict within you. You may find that it is not very popular to be a believer in Jesus. I hope that this will not happen, but some of your friends may not want to be associated with you anymore.

All men will hate you because of me. Luke 21:17

People are typically afraid of what they do not understand. The best thing you can do is show patients and continue to be kind to them by nurturing a new relationship with Jesus in the center of the whole situation.

You would be surprised how many of my friends were won to Jesus by kindness in our friendships. Even though they might say harsh things about you or be unkind, doing the right thing is always best. Remember kindness in most cases will diffuse anger and misunderstanding.

An anxious heart weighs a man down, but a kind word cheers him up. Proverbs 12:25

A gentle answer turns away wrath, but a harsh word stirs up anger. Proverbs 15:1

GROWING FRUIT

Let us be honest, it is very tough to suddenly change your lifestyle. However, as I said earlier this would take time as the Holy Spirit begins to change you. On this journey, you will make mistakes – lots of them.

When this happens, confess it to God and turn from that behavior. This is called repenting. God gives you grace when this happens. He is not some taskmaster just waiting to pounce on you when you mess up. When fear is present, it is very difficult for you to understand just how much God really loves you. One of the most effective weapons satan has is to get you to doubt your relationship with God.

Knowing the truth about who you are in Jesus corrects your spiritual perspective. You will then know who Jesus made you to be. If you follow the leading of the Holy Spirit He will renew your thinking to the way God thinks about you. You will be amazed at how God starts working in your life. You are no longer bound to the desires of your sinful nature. You start loving people with a love that only God can give. There is a new joy and inner peace in your life. You start finding that you are much more patient with people and confident in the decisions you make daily.

All these things are called the fruits of the Spirit. You may not fully understand it, but know that all these characteristics are the personality of the Holy Spirit working in your life. It is remarkable to see this happening totally against your former nature and manner. God loves doing that in and for us. He is shaping us to become more like Jesus.

But the fruit of the Spirit is love, joy, peace, patience, kindness, goodness, faithfulness, gentleness and self-control. Against such things there is no law. Those who belong to Christ Jesus have crucified the sinful nature with its passions and desires. Since we live by the Spirit, let us keep in step with the Spirit. Let us not become conceited, provoking and envying each other. Galatians 5: 22-26

LEGALISM & RELIGION

It is possible that you will experience legalism (strict rules) at a church. Legalism is adding additional requirements to gain favor in the eyes of God. There are rules for the way you dress, the way you worship, your friendships even which Bible you study. This approach to Christian living lacks the grace to live and strive with one another. You cannot do anything to make God love you more. Legalism and religion go hand-in-hand and it is one of the mindsets (ways of thinking) in the church today. This mindset is the number one enemy of the cross. Legalism in a church is a cancerous thing. It brings about an unhealthy view of God and in our relationship with Him.

"Woe to you, teachers of the law and Pharisees, you hypocrites! You give a tenth of your spices—mint, dill and cummin. But you have neglected the more important matters of the law—justice, mercy and faithfulness. You should have practiced the latter, without neglecting the former. Matthew 23:23

I do not set aside the grace of God, for if righteousness could be gained through the law, Christ died for nothing!" Galatians 2:21

For the law was given through Moses; grace and truth came through Jesus Christ. John 1:17

Before he became a believer, the Apostle Paul was one of the most devout legalists and religious leaders who ever lived. This man was very well educated and entrenched in the tradition of legalism. Paul was a loyal Jew who received orders from government officials to hunt down, torture, and kill Christians. It is impossible to gain God's love by following a bunch of rules we cannot possibly live up to.

"I too was convinced that I ought to do all that was possible to oppose the name of Jesus of Nazareth. And that is just what I did in Jerusalem. On the authority of the chief priests I put many of the saints in prison, and

when they were put to death, I cast my vote against them.
Acts 9-10

Someone who has this mindset will find it very difficult to admit when they are wrong. This is nothing more than self-righteous pride.

Have you ever done something wrong and then felt like you had to "feel bad" for a period before you can accept forgiveness for your sin? Once you repent of a failure, you must instantly accept and believe the truth about the Blood of Jesus washing that sin away. The very moment you repent of your sin, God forgives you. He does not withhold forgiveness for even a fraction of a second. Your sin is forgiven immediately!

That if you confess with your mouth, "Jesus is Lord," and believe in your heart that God raised him from the dead, you will be saved. Romans 10:9

God is concerned with the condition of your heart more than any outward appearances or works. Unfortunately, many Christians have a false notion that they need to do more and more to make God love them, or to keep His love and approval. The Bible makes it clear that Jesus loves us for who we are, not because of what we are, or anything we have done. He is not a respecter of persons. He does not show favoritism because He loves everyone the same.

Then Peter began to speak: "I now realize how true it is that God does not show favoritism, but accepts men from every nation who fear him and do what is right." Acts 10:34-35

I remember when we moved to Grand Forks, North Dakota. We were new in town and invited to attend church at an old friend's request. My boys were young then and liked to wear colored laces in their tennis shoes. When we got to church that morning, I could instantly sense that we were underdressed. Everyone there was wearing a three-piece suite and the women were all wearing long modest dresses.

We received some of the oddest looks of disapproval I had ever seen. We were also questioned about the version of the Bible we were using. Unfortunately, we were not invited back. No church is perfect, but we must realize that when man gets involved with church, you have rules. When the Holy Spirit leads the church, there is liberty, freedom and grace for one another.

All of you, clothe yourselves with humility toward one another, because, "God opposes the proud but gives grace to the humble." 1 Peter 5:5

JUST THE FACTS:
- ✓ Always do the right thing by being kind to others.
- ✓ Win your friends with the love of God.
- ✓ God is not a taskmaster.
- ✓ You cannot earn God's love.
- ✓ Accept people for who they are without judgment.

Chapter 6
HERE FOR A REASON

As the body of Christ, we are considered His ambassadors. An ambassador is somebody who represents another person, group or nation. We as believers are supposed to be representing Jesus here on earth today.

We are therefore Christ's ambassadors, as though God were making his appeal through us. We implore you on Christ's behalf: Be reconciled to God. 2 Corinthians 5:20

Being an ambassador for Jesus not only requires a commitment on our part, but it is a command. This is a huge responsibility. That means that we are to go forward doing His work here on earth the way He demonstrated to us by His example. Non-believers see and judge us by the way we live. (Witness)

Again Jesus said, "Peace be with you! As the Father has sent me, I am sending you." John 20:21

Then Jesus came to them and said, "All authority in heaven and on earth has been given to me. Therefore go and make disciples of all nations, baptizing them in the name of the Father and of the Son and of the Holy Spirit. Matthew 28:18-19

THE GOLDEN RULE

Often times it is very difficult to love or even like people. It would appear that in this world people are concerned about him or herself more than anyone else is. Those that are not very likeable are really just acting out of what they know. Unbelievers act out of the flesh, the sinful nature, because they do not have the indwelling Holy Spirit that changes them. They are lost and do not realize what they could become in Jesus.

It is very easy to get upset when someone does you wrong. Often our first inclination is to act out of the old nature and retaliate or get even. This would be sinning by repaying evil with evil, but overcome it with good. Instead, we are to do the more difficult thing. That is to turn their attack into a blessing by acting toward them in kindness. You might be surprised at how your kind act diffuses someone's anger. The Lord will bless you as you respond in kindness because He said He would. Nevertheless, remember, when you endure personal attack for doing what is right, God will reward you for your good work. Do not be worried about threats, but continue to honor the Lord with the way you live.

Finally, all of you, live in harmony with one another; be sympathetic, love as brothers, be compassionate and humble. Do not repay evil with evil or insult with insult, but with blessing, because to this you were called so that you may inherit a blessing. 1 Peter 3: 8-9

If you really keep the royal law found in Scripture, "Love your neighbor as yourself," you are doing right. James 2:8

WE ARE HIS WORKMANSHIP

You may not believe or understand this at first, but you are the workmanship of God. Just as a painter is inspired to paint a portrait or landscape, many thoughts are given as to the approach to create. As the painter starts to paint there is a canvas on which the artist fashions or creates the painting. This canvas represents life. As the artist progresses through his workmanship, every color and stroke of the brush adds another element of inspired creation. God did the same thing when He made you. We are created in God's image.

God's plan for His people includes a "walk," or journey through life in good works. The Christian's whole life is a work of God. Paul said, "We are His workmanship," a word from which we get our English word "poem." The life of His people is God's poetic work of art.

This includes every believer in Christ! God wonderfully made you and me! That's incredible.

For we are God's workmanship, created in Christ Jesus to do good works, which God prepared in advance for us to do. Ephesians 2:10

I praise you because I am fearfully and wonderfully made; your works are wonderful, I know that full well. Psalm 139:14

As we walk through life, God is continually brushing strokes and creating the paths on which we are to walk and serve. He said that He has prepared these paths since the beginning of time before we were even born. You see, God wants us to live the good life, which He prearranged and made ready for us to live. His ultimate purpose is for us as His creation, to bring Him glory. *Psalms 23:3 says; He guides me in paths of righteousness for His namesake.* You see it is not for our sake but His. In return, God gives us fullness of life and eternal security through His son Jesus Christ.

JUST THE FACTS:
- ✓ We represent Jesus to the world.
- ✓ Life is fleeting in relation to eternity.
- ✓ Do not repay evil with evil; overcome it with good.
- ✓ God created you for a purpose.

My Thoughts:

Chapter 7
PUTTING ON THE ARMOR

Just as a soldier readies himself for battle, we are to do the same as followers of Jesus. We are now soldiers in the Lord's army. We are not battling against flesh and blood but against powers beyond the physical. The battle is against the master spirits that control the world rulers of the present darkness on earth. You see, there are forces of wickedness in the supernatural sphere that will come against everything that is of God, including you.

Although he is not willing to concede, satan is a defeated foe. He knows that the battle of good and evil was won on the cross with the shed blood of Jesus. The plan satan orchestrated in the Garden of Eden, which led to the sinful disobedience of Adam and Eve, was set straight when Jesus went to the cross. It is satan's plan to use a strategy of deception to lead us astray and to get us to doubt our faith.

It is so important that each one of us be ready for battle. Just as a soldier depends on his personal equipment and weapons for self-preservation, we to must be familiar with the equipment God has given us as well. It is God's intention that we be prepared for battle and forcefully take back territory lost to the enemy (satan).

For our struggle is not against flesh and blood, but against the rulers, against the authorities, against the powers of this dark world and against the spiritual forces of evil in the heavenly realms. Ephesians 6:12

From the days of John the Baptist until now, the kingdom of heaven has been forcefully advancing, and forceful men lay hold of it. Matthew 11:12

THE WHOLE ARMOR

The armor we put on can be described by one word, which has come over into English as "panoply." It is the total equipment of the soldier, both offensive and defensive. This is similar to putting on the new nature described in Ephesians 4:24. This equipment enables the Christian soldier to stand against the enemy, who is the devil, already mentioned as a present danger in Ephesians 4:27. The activities of satan are described as clever and subtle in Ephesians 4:14.

and to be made new in the attitudes of your minds; and to put on the new self, created to be like God in true righteousness and holiness. Ephesians 4:23-24

***and do not give the devil a foothold.* Ephesians 4:27**

The apostle Paul stressed that the enemy is more than human. There is a staggering lineup of spiritual forces and their human agents who war against God and His people. Many teachers are quick to dismiss such a vision of supernatural evil, but man has not been able to dismiss the power of evil over his life so easily. The warning Paul gives needs to be taken seriously. Due to this conflict with evil, Paul repeated his challenge to take up the armor of God, and to "stand". Standing speaks of both stability and victory.

THE BELT OF TRUTH

The first step in preparing for battle was to gird up the loins. Men in ancient times wore long robes. These could hinder movement, so for work or battle, they were pulled up and tied about the waist and hips with a girdle or belt. The belt in this case represents the "truth", meaning sincerity and integrity of character. According to the Gospel, the idea of truth is included in the items of shoes and sword. The Christian who goes to fight against the lies of the devil must not be tripped up by any untruth in their own life.

YOUR BREASTPLATE

The breastplate is vital for protecting the heart. It represents the "righteousness" of a Christian. This piece of equipment is the basic defense against evil. You must be obedient to God's will and upright in your own conduct. Wrong attitudes and actions leave openings and become weak spots in the armor through which the enemy thrusts his weapons.

He put on righteousness as his breastplate. Isaiah 59:17

YOUR SHOES

Shoes were also important, as every foot soldier soon learns. Shoes that pinch, slip, or weigh down the step may make a crucial difference in the battle. For the Christian soldier, it is the "Gospel of peace" that makes his feet spring lightly across the field. Paul, like Isaiah, emphasized the feet of those who bring good news.

How beautiful on the mountains are the feet of those who bring good news, who proclaim peace, who bring good tidings, who proclaim salvation, who say to Zion, "Your God reigns!" Isaiah 52:7

And how can they preach unless they are sent? As it is written, "How beautiful are the feet of those who bring good news!" Romans 10:15

THE SHIELD

The shield is the whole body, about two and one-half by four feet in size. Made of leather and sometimes soaked in water, it could protect from the flaming arrows which burn as well as pierce. The Christian's shield is "faith", the complete confidence he has in God's power. This willingness to let God's power work in our lives can counter everything the enemy throws at us. The "taking" described here is not grabbing with our own strength but receiving what is given.

In addition to all this, take up the shield of faith, with which you can extinguish all the flaming arrows of the evil one. Ephesians 6:16

THE HELMET

The helmet protects the most vital and vulnerable part of all, the head or mind. "Salvation" is the Christian's most basic protection due to God's grace and the guarantee of eternal life. Nothing the enemy can do will break through the bond that holds you to God. Regardless of setbacks, when the battle is over, your head will be held high.

Take the helmet of salvation and the sword of the Spirit, which is the word of God. Ephesians 6:17

THE SWORD

The sword is the only offensive weapon included here. The Christian is ready to attack as well as defend. His sword is provided by the Spirit. It's God's weapon, the only one adequate for a spiritual battle; the "Word" of God is His sword. This refers to God's message, whether spoken or written. Christ is the personal Word of God and He himself wields the sword against the forces of evil.

From his mouth came a sharp sword to strike down the nations. He will rule them with an iron rod. He will release the fierce wrath of God, the Almighty, like juice flowing from a winepress. **Revelation 19:15**

JUST THE FACTS:
- ✓ We are soldiers in God's army.
- ✓ Recognize satan's plan to deceive.
- ✓ Wear the armor to fight the battles.
- ✓ Press forward taking territory for the kingdom.

My Thoughts:

Chapter 8
KEYS TO FAITH

While writing this chapter, I was listening to Dr. Dobson from Focus on The Family interview Steven Curtis Chapman. He shared the tragic story about the loss of his daughter Maria. Steven was asked if he was angry at God. He said absolutely not! He did say however, that he is angry with satan. That may sound strange, but you see Steven is fully aware of the spiritual realm that exists and that satan is the one who looks to kill, steal and destroy.

It is important to understand that satan is the one who afflicts and creates hardship. Faith is trusting in God and a lack of faith is doubt. At times you may feel like God has left you, but He never will. God said He would never leave nor forsake us. God is always right there beside you. In times of hopelessness all you need to do is reach out your hand.

THE KEYS

There are *three basic keys* to hold on to concerning Biblical faith. When you combine these three elements and put them into practice, you will operate in great power, moving the mountains in life!

In Mark 9, there was a boy that had an unclean spirit, such a strong unclean spirit that even Jesus' disciples could not cast it out. They were deliverance pastors going about setting people free from bondage regularly, but for some reason when they came across this boy, they were not able to.

A man in the crowd answered, "Teacher, I brought you my son, who is possessed by a spirit that has robbed him of speech. Whenever it seizes him, it throws him to the ground. He foams at the mouth, gnashes his teeth and becomes rigid. I asked your disciples to drive out the spirit, but they could not." Mark 9:17-18

Now Jesus gave His disciples authority over all powers of the enemy and they knew His authority was real.

I have given you authority to trample on snakes and scorpions and to overcome all the power of the enemy; nothing will harm you. Luke 10:19

So what did these disciples lack? Clearly, they did not lack authority! What they did lack was faith in that authority.

"O unbelieving generation," Jesus replied, "how long shall I stay with you? How long shall I put up with you? Bring the boy to me." Mark 9:19

This story was told in Matthew 17 as well. When they asked Jesus why they were unable to cast out the evil spirit, Jesus told them flat out, "You lacked faith!

Then the disciples came to Jesus in private and asked, "Why couldn't we drive it out?"

He replied, "Because you have so little faith. I tell you the truth, if you have faith as small as a mustard seed, you can say to this mountain, 'Move from here to there' and it will move. Nothing will be impossible for you." Matthew 17: 19-20

In the above verse, we see that Jesus told us to speak <u>to</u> the mountains of life, not about them. Never waiver on God's Word and always take hold of His promises! If He said we would cast out demons, then it means He has given us the authority to do so. If He said we have a right to be healed in Jesus' name, then we have that right. If He says to speak to the mountain, it will move.

God increases our faith through the outpouring of His favor as we serve and minister to others. Remember, faith dominates doubt and in its place comes the presence of belief. Christian faith is taking God for His Word and believing the promises He has made.

Do not try to examine your faith. Why? Because in doing so, you are allowing an opportunity for doubts to enter the mind. It gives satan an open door to deceive and plant seeds of doubt.

Faith is the assurance, confirmation, the title deed of the things we hope for, being the proof of things we do not see and the conviction of their reality. Faith perceives as real fact what is not revealed to our natural senses.

What does that mean? Let me explain. It is important to first know what hope is. The worldview sees hope as something that may happen, a possibility that something may happen. It is fleeting at best without any confirmed expectation. This is because those without the indwelling Holy Spirit have no eternal hope!

Brothers, we do not want you to be ignorant about those who fall asleep, or to grieve like the rest of men, who have no hope. Thessalonians 4:13

Christians have the greatest hope of all. We have salvation in Jesus and look forward to His return! It is because of this great hope, that we have the excited joyful expectation of sometime good! You will know a Christian who has great faith by the measure of joy in their life. You just want to be around them! They draw people to themselves by the joy of the indwelling Spirit of God.

Faith Key #1: Knowledge Brings Faith

Knowledge of the truth in God's Word brings faith. The new age movement teaches that we can "believe things into existence," which is not the same kind of faith that

The Simple Truth: At times in your Christian walk, you might feel like you do not have great faith. Just know that it is satan who wants to destroy your faith in God. If he can do that, he has employed one of his most deceptive tools. There is a spiritual realm we must contend with. You can be sure of this one important thing. Greater is the Holy Spirit within you, than the unholy spirits that rule this world. If God is with you, nothing can stand against you!

Christians should have. Our faith is based upon the truth in God's Word. Thus, knowing what God's Word has to say about something gives us the ability to believe it.

For example, how can you have faith to pray for a healing, believing that He will heal you, if you did not know it was God's will for your healing? This is why satan works so hard to tell the church today that it may not be God's will for them to be healed! Why? Because it casts doubt, the opposite of faith, upon the hearts of God's children! How can you grasp the promises of God, if you do not know what they are? We must first know the truth and then believe it. That is Biblical faith!

'If you can'?" said Jesus. "Everything is possible for him who believes." Mark 9:23

In the verse above, the word "believes" means to trust. Jesus was in essence telling His disciples that all things referring to the promises of God are possible for them who will trust God.

How can you believe something that nobody told you? You cannot. That is why it is important to know what the Word of God says, so we can believe it. Faith comes by hearing the Word of God.

Consequently, faith comes from hearing the message, and the message is heard through the word of Christ. **Romans 10:17**

Faith key #2: Faith and a Pure Conscience

There is a definite connection between a clean conscience and faith. You must know you are clean spiritually, because your faith depends on it. How can you confidently approach God, when your conscience is guilty? The truth is you cannot!

let us draw near to God with a sincere heart in full assurance of faith, having our hearts sprinkled to cleanse us from a guilty conscience and having our bodies washed with pure water. **Hebrews 10:22**

We need to have a true heart washed clean from a guilty conscience when we approach God.

Faith key #3: Faith Works Through Love

The third key to operating in faith is rooted and grounded in love so your faith will operate through love. The Bible tells us clearly that all believers should be rooted and grounded in the love of Christ. If you want to experience the fullness of God who is able to do exceedingly abundant above all that we ask or think, His love in us is essential.

I pray that out of his glorious riches he may strengthen you with power through his Spirit in your inner being, so that Christ may dwell in your hearts through faith. And I pray that you, being rooted and established in love, may have power, together with all the saints, to grasp how wide and long and high and deep is the love of Christ, and to know this love that surpasses knowledge—that you may be filled to the measure of all the fullness of God.

Now to him who is able to do immeasurably more than all we ask or imagine, according to his power that is at work within us. Ephesians 3:16-20

We are told to put on the breastplate of faith and love. They go together like hand and glove!

But since we belong to the day, let us be self-controlled, putting on faith and love as a breastplate, and the hope of salvation as a helmet. 1 Thessalonians 5:8

As we follow Jesus and walk by the leading of the Holy Spirit, love will begin to flow through us giving increase to our faith. Among the fruits of the Spirit, we find both faith and love.

But the fruit of the Spirit is love, joy, peace, patience, kindness, goodness, faithfulness, gentleness and self-control. Against such things there is no law. Those who belong to Christ Jesus have crucified the sinful nature with its passions and desires. Since we live by the Spirit, let us keep in step with the Spirit. Let us not become conceited, provoking and envying each other. **Galatians 5:22-33**

For in Christ Jesus neither circumcision nor uncircumcision has any value. The only thing that counts is faith expressing itself through love. **Galatians 5:6**

A HINDERANCE TO FAITH

One of the greatest hindrances to faith is strongholds. Things like hate, bitterness, and anger can create these holds on us. If strongholds influence us, we will have a very difficult time believing God for something. For example, if you see God as cruel and distant, how can you believe it is really His will to heal and bless you? Strongholds can be devastating to our faith!

Knowing the truth about who you are in Jesus resets the self-perspective from how you see yourself, to who Jesus has made you to be. Once you know this truth, your inner spirit comes into alignment with the (truth) provision of God.

Then you will know the truth, and the truth will set you free." John 8:32

> JUST THE FACTS:
> ✓ You have power and authority over all evil.
> ✓ Your faith in Jesus is the key to moving mountains.
> ✓ Study the Bible and apply the truth.
> ✓ Do not let strongholds hinder your relationship with Jesus.

My Thoughts:

Chapter 9
THE HOUR OF TRIAL

The life we live while here on earth is not all there is. As I mentioned earlier, our time here is a preparation for what is to come. Christians are but pilgrims in a strange and foreign land. We are here for a limited time only. While here, we are considered as aliens and strangers exiled in this world. The Bible says that life here on earth is but a mist that appears for a little while and then we are gone. There is so much more to look forward to in the expanse of eternity.

While here, we are to continually grow in our faith and pursue the things of God. We continually run the race just as an Olympic Athlete prepares for the big event. It is a growth process in every aspect of our life.

Life is fine-tuning and sharpening our gifts while we depend on and tap into the power of God for ministry. God is preparing us for bigger and better things that will assist us as we serve the eternal kingdom.

Why, you do not even know what will happen tomorrow. What is your life? You are a mist that appears for a little while and then vanishes. James 4:14

Dear friends, I urge you, as aliens and strangers in the world, to abstain from sinful desires, which war against your soul.
1 Peter 2

WATCH THE PROMISED LAND

Jesus knew when His death on the cross was finished, satan would be to. Now it is just a matter of time before Jesus returns for His chosen. He will rule and reign on earth as the King of Kings and the Lord of Lords over all governments and kingdoms.

Jesus will return for His church as a groom comes for His soon to be bride. The trumpet of God will sound and those who were dead in Christ will be raised from the dead imperishable and without decay. Then we who are alive will be caught up to meet Him in the clouds. I believe this is when the tribulation period of seven years will start.

For the Lord himself will come down from heaven, with a loud command, with the voice of the archangel and with the trumpet call of God, and the dead in Christ will rise first. 1 Thessalonians 4:16

WHAT'S A RAPTURE?

The word "rapture" does not appear in the Bible anywhere. It refers to a catching away of the church. You will hear this term often as you walk in your new Christian faith. There are many theories introduced by scholars about the catching away described in the Bible.

The seven-year period is a time span in this current church age. During this time, the anti-christ and the false prophet will control world governments and religion on the earth. This is a time of great trail, pestilence and suffering for those unbelievers left behind. The Bible says that no man knows the hour in which this "catching away" of the church will occur except the Father in heaven. However, we can look at the seasons and the fulfillment of prophetic events in this present time, to know when it approaches.

The prelude to this one world government is represented today in the currently developing European Union. Moreover, the institution of a one-world currency will facilitate a one-world government. Eventually, currency will become outdated in this digital age. The book of revelation speaks of the "mark" of the beast. This mark will most likely be a tattooed bar code, "the number" of the beast, on the forehead or back of the hand. The possibility of an implanted microchip is also likely. Today there is a microchip developed for this very purpose and is being used in pets for veterinary data, identification and GPS location.

It has even been tested on humans. Scripture says that people living in this period will not be able to buy or sell without the mark of the beast.

and he provides that no one will be able to buy or to sell, except the one who has the mark, either the name of the beast or the number of his name. Revelation 13:17

"And the smoke of their torment goes up forever and ever; they have no rest day and night, those who worship the beast and his image, and whoever receives the mark of his name." Revelation 14:11

So the first angel went and poured out his bowl on the earth; and it became a loathsome and malignant sore on the people who had the mark of the beast and who worshiped his image. Revelation 16:2

Then I saw thrones, and they sat on them, and judgment was given to them And I saw the souls of those who had been beheaded because of their testimony of Jesus and because of the word of God, and those who had not worshiped the beast or his image, and had not received the mark on their forehead and on their hand; and they came to life and reigned with Christ for a thousand years. Revelation 20:4

This is a very deep and complex subject area of scripture, especially for new believers. I will just scratch the surface in an attempt to show the different perspectives on when the "rapture" will occur. The following is present day theories of this occurrence.

Pre-Tribulation Rapture: (or "pre-trib")

The Rapture of the saints happens just before the seven year Tribulation, so that believers will not have to experience any of its disruption and pain. Supporters of the "pre-trib" position suggest that Jesus will have three comings: the first during the first century, the second at the start of the tribulation, and a third at the end of the tribulation.

Post-tribulation Rapture: (or "post-trib")

The faithful will experience the full horrors of the entire Tribulation and are raptured only at the end of the 7 years. The main problem with this theory is that there are many Bible passages, which state that Jesus return will be at a time that cannot be predicted. Nevertheless, the Tribulation period starts with the arrival of the Antichrist and an interval of peace. Precisely, 42 months later, a sudden shift occurs, a peace treaty with Israel is broken, and devastation begins.

Mid-Tribulation Rapture: (or "mid-trib")

The Rapture happens 42 months into the Tribulation. Up to that time, the Antichrist brings peace to the world. After 42 months, events take a sudden turn for the worse. Some supporters of the "mid-trib" position suggest that there will be many mini-raptures.

Pre-wrath Rapture:

This is a new theory, promoted by Marvin Rosenthal, former director of Friends of Israel, and others. Their view teaches that the church must experience most of the Tribulation, and then be raptured towards the end of the Tribulation period.

Partial Rapture:

This theory teaches that the faithful born-again believers are raptured just before the Tribulation. Newly born again believers are raptured during or at the end of the Tribulation.

Regardless of which position you take, I believe Scripture teaches clearly that believers will be kept from the *"hour of trial"* which God will send upon the world to test unbelievers.

Since you have kept my command to endure patiently, I will <u>also keep you from the hour of trial</u> that is going to come upon the whole world to test those who live on the earth. Revelation 3:10

"At that time Michael, the great prince who protects your people, will arise. There will be a time of distress such as has not happened from the beginning of nations until then. <u>But at that time your people—everyone whose name is found written in the book—will be delivered.</u> Multitudes who sleep in the dust of the earth will awake: some to everlasting life, others to shame and everlasting contempt. Daniel 12: 1-2

Part of the confusion is that there is a failure to distinguish the "two stages" in Jesus' second coming. One passage speaks of Jesus coming in the "air" and in the "secret", like a thief coming in the night for His bride "the church." The other describes Christ's coming in power and majesty to the earth, with every eye seeing His return.

For the Lord himself will come down from heaven, with a loud command, with the voice of the archangel and with the trumpet call of God, and the dead in Christ will rise first. After that, we who are still alive and are left will be caught up together with them in the clouds to meet the Lord in the air. And so we will be with the Lord forever. 1 Thessalonians 4: 16-17

for you know very well that the day of the Lord will come like a thief in the night. 1 Thessalonians 5:2

The Lord's return in secret can be compared with the Jewish tradition of a man coming for his bride. He does this without announcement and in secret to whisk her away. Jesus refers to the body of believers as His bride. I believe this will occur before the tribulation period. God will not allow His bride to endure the trial to come.

As a young man marries a maiden, so will your sons marry you; as a bridegroom rejoices over his bride, so will your God rejoice over you. Isaiah 62:5

THE CHURCH AGE

We are currently living in the New Testament church age, the time of the Gentiles. In this age, we are to go into the entire world to teach and preach the gospel to all people. We will do this until the time of the Gentiles has been fulfilled. Jesus passed this responsibility on to the Gentiles because the Jewish people clearly rejected Him. God's original intention was for the people of Israel to press forward with this commission as well.

For this reason they could not believe, because, as Isaiah says elsewhere: "He has blinded their eyes and deadened their hearts, so they can neither see with their eyes, nor understand with their hearts, nor turn—and I would heal them." John 12: 39-40

However, God knew the Jewish people would reject His son. As a result, He will show His people what could have been and what was meant for them in the great commission. You see, right now God has blinded their eyes to the truth of their Messiah due to their rejection of Him. Even so, when the time of the Gentiles is fulfilled, God will lift their blindness, and they will suffer great sorrow knowing finally the truth of what they have done. They expected the Messiah to come with great power in their day, not as a child born in a manger or the son of a carpenter.

What is interesting to note, is that the people of Israel once again became a sovereign nation on May 15, 1948. This is a major fulfillment of a prophecy that marks the beginning of the *end of this age*. It was also prophesied that the tribes of Israel scattered for thousands of years would once again return to their homeland from all over the globe. This is happening today!

> *The Simple Truth: Jesus is coming back for His bride. The blessed hope we have in Christ out ways any circumstance we can live in. As I said earlier, the Bible is active and alive. Although many may speculate on the return of Christ, rest assured God is in control.*

He will raise a banner for the nations and gather the exiles of Israel; he will assemble the scattered people of Judah from the four quarters of the earth. Isaiah 11:12

I will bring back my exiled people Israel; they will rebuild the ruined cities and live in them. They will plant vineyards and drink their wine; they will make gardens and eat their fruit. Amos 9:14

Isaiah wrote God's words of comfort for His people in chapter 40 and said, **but those who hope in the LORD will renew their strength. They will soar <u>on wings like eagles</u>; they will run and not grow weary, they will walk and not be faint.**

Today there is an organization called "On Wings of Eagles." Their sole purpose is to fly the scattered Jewish people back to their homeland, Israel.

As you can see, there is much yet to be fulfilled in God's plan for the future. I hope this stirred an interest in what's happening in the world today. The future is foretold in the Bible. I merely touched the surface of this subject.

If you are interested in further study, I highly recommend the book "There is a New World Coming" by Hal Lindsey. He does an excellent job of explaining all facets of this fascinating subject. I can guarantee you will never look at world events as you once did.

You may have noticed that this book was written with much simplicity as I stated before. This was purposefully done for the understanding of the new Christian. All of these areas addressed questions I once had when I first received Jesus as my Savior as well.

We are living during an exciting time in history. The Bible is coming alive in front of our eyes. I believe we are about to see God move in a powerful way in the next few years. He is ***reigniting*** the excitement and power experienced during the early church in this present day. He chose us, for this great privilege.

I want to encourage each of you to continually press into your new relationship with Jesus. Study your Bible and don't be afraid to seek out wise Godly counsel. I pray that God will grant you the deepest desires of your heart as you continually pursue Him.

JUST THE FACTS:
- ✓ We are the bride of Christ Jesus.
- ✓ Jesus is coming back for us as the King of king's and the Lord of lords.
- ✓ Always pursue the higher calling of God.
- ✓ Pray for and support the people of Israel.

My Thoughts:

REFERENCE BIBLIOGRAPHY

God's Word: New International Version HOLY BIBLE. Copyright© 1973, 1978, 1984 by International Bible Society: by permission.

Reasons To Believe: http://www.reasons.org (Accessed 30 Aug 2008)

Great Bible Studies; Copyrighted © 2003-2008 Pastor Robert L.: by permission.

RECOMMENDED BOOKS

RELEASING THE HOLY SPIRIT
THE MINISTERING MESSIAH
A GLOW OF GODLINESS
THE KINGDOM WITHIN
A GLOBAL AWAKENING
MONEY BASICS

ORDER AT:
https://sites.google.com/site/micksgbooks

Made in the USA
Columbia, SC
23 December 2021